SEEING INTO TOMORROW

HAIKU BY **Richard Wright**

BIOGRAPHY AND ILLUSTRATIONS BY **Nina Crews**

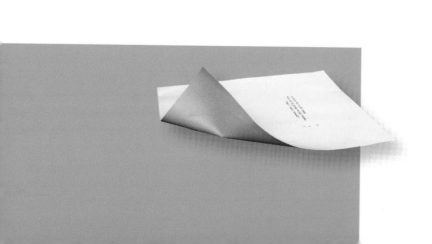

M MILLBROOK PRESS · MINNEAPOLIS

FOR MY FAMILY, WHO SHOWED ME THE WAY —N.C.

Thank you to Michael Allen, Asa Antoine, Donald Crews, Jeremy Dorval-Moller, Jadari Georges, Devin Hollingsworth, Julian Kakalec, Michael Kanyongolo, Bayo Maathey, Joshua Mirob, Gus Rader, and Jackson-Leroi Widoff-Woodson for posing for the illustrations in this book.

Millbrook Press
A division of Lerner Publishing Group, Inc.
241 First Avenue North
Minneapolis, MN 55401 USA

For reading levels and more information, look up this title at www.lernerbooks.com.

Additional image on p. 3 courtesy of Yale Collection of American Literature, Beinecke Rare Book and Manuscript Library.

Main body text set in Johnston ITC Std Bold 22/30.
Typeface provided by International Typeface Corporation.
The illustrations for this book are created from 35mm digital photographs collaged and manipulated in Adobe Photoshop.

Library of Congress Cataloging-in-Publication Data

Names: Wright, Richard, 1908–1960, author. | Crews, Nina, illustrator.
Title: Seeing into tomorrow : haiku by Richard Wright / illustrated by Nina Crews.
Description: Minneapolis : Millbrook Press, 2018. | Includes bibliographical references.
Identifiers: LCCN 2017016951 (print) | LCCN 2017031042 (ebook) | ISBN 9781512498622 (eb pdf) | ISBN 9781512418651 (lb : alk. paper)
Subjects: LCSH: Haiku, American. | Wright, Richard, 1908–1960—Juvenile literature.
Classification: LCC PS3545.R815 (ebook) | LCC PS3545.R815 A6 2018 (print) | DDC 811/.52—dc23

LC record available at https://lccn.loc.gov/2017016951

Manufactured in the United States of America
1-41234-23230-7/7/2017

The poems in this book were written by a man named Richard Wright.
When Richard was a child in Mississippi, he did not know he would grow up to be a famous writer. He was a little boy who knew the sound of trees rustling in the wind, the journey of a solitary ant, and the brown of a muddy dirt road. Richard grew up in a time and a place when many people said that brown little boys like him didn't grow up to be famous writers. But he did. Richard Wright wrote stories, novels, essays, plays, and poems known all over the world. And I would guess that one of the first words he wrote was his name.

Just enough of snow

For a boy's finger to write

His name on the porch.

As my delegate,

My shadow imitates me

This first day of spring.

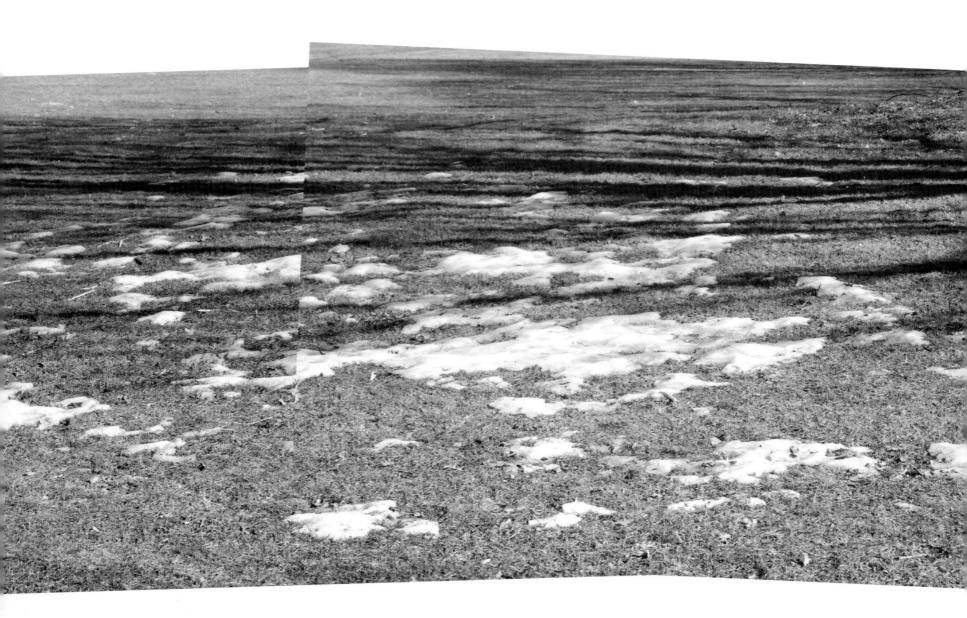

Is this the dirt road,

Winding
through
windy
trees,

That I must travel?

So insistently

A crow caws in a spring field

That I want to look.

Under a low sky

A boy walking with a dog

In the spring rain.

The clouds are smiling

At a single yellow kite

Swaying

under

them.

Empty railroad tracks:

A train sounds in the spring hills

And the rails leap with life.

A loud ticking clock

Sounds in rhythm with the heat

Of a long slow day.

Suddenly mindful,

The tree was looking at me,

Each green leaf alive.

"Say, Mr. Beetle,

Are you taking a detour

Crawling on my knee?"

As day tumbles down,

The setting sun's signature

Is written in red.

A spring sky so clear

That you feel you are seeing

Into tomorrow.

THE HAIKU YOU HAVE JUST READ ARE TWELVE OF MORE THAN FOUR THOUSAND WRITTEN BY RICHARD WRIGHT.

Haiku poems originated in Japan. Most haiku, including the ones in this book, have five syllables in the first line, seven syllables in the second line, and five syllables in the third. They typically don't rhyme. Traditional haiku describe something or someplace in nature at a specific time—a moment. Through this description, a feeling such as happiness, sadness, loneliness, or anger may be expressed, but it is rarely named directly.

RICHARD WRIGHT WAS ONE OF THE IMPORTANT AFRICAN AMERICAN WRITERS OF THE TWENTIETH CENTURY. He is known for his writing about the suffering caused by racism and about struggles for freedom in the United States and around the world. When I first read these poems, I wondered what inspired Wright to write about nature and the seasons. I found out that he wrote them at a time that he described himself as being "even more sensitive than usual." Perhaps that made the places and things he saw every day look new and inspiring. The poems are also tied to his memories of being a young boy in the countryside. Memories of days passing slowly, of finding magic in watching ants in the grass, clouds in the sky, and geese and sparrows flying far above.

Richard Wright was born in 1908. His family lived on a farm. They were very poor. His father, Nathan Wright, was a sharecropper. Sharecroppers were farmers who rented land from other farmers. They often owed the landowner more money than they could earn from the crops they grew. His mother, Ella, had been a schoolteacher, but she stopped working to raise Richard and his younger brother, Leon. Nathan left the family when Richard was quite young. Ella struggled to support herself and the boys, but she was often ill and could not work. They sometimes lived with her relatives, and Ella briefly put Richard and Leon in an orphanage when she had no means to support them.

Food was always scarce for Richard's family and he often didn't have enough to eat. Despite that, his greatest hunger was for knowledge. Because his family moved often, Richard was in and out of school. He was very bright, and when he went to school, he excelled. He loved books and aspired to be a writer. He published his first story in a black newspaper when he was still a teenager. The story was inspired by the detective stories he liked to read.

Richard left Mississippi as a young man and went to the North, like many African Americans at that time, following promises of better job opportunities and freedom from segregation. He got his start as a writer in Chicago and eventually moved to New York City. While there, he wrote his best-known books: *Uncle Tom's Children*, *Native Son*, and, his autobiography, *Black Boy*. *Native Son* and *Black Boy* were best sellers and were widely read and discussed. Although the success of his books made Richard famous, he kept moving because fame could not protect him from the sting of prejudice in his daily life. He heard that circumstances were better for African Americans in Europe, so he moved to Paris, France, with his wife and daughter in 1947.

In Paris, the Wrights had another daughter. Richard made friends with many writers, artists, and intellectuals and was inspired by them. He wrote more novels, essays, and plays. He traveled to Spain, Indonesia, and Ghana and wrote about the struggles for freedom in those countries. In 1959, while Richard and his family were vacationing in the French countryside, he started writing haiku. His writing had not been going well and his health was poor, so perhaps it was a good time to try something new. He wrote about things he observed and things he remembered. He read his haiku aloud to his teenage daughter and encouraged her to write them too. Then Richard sorted through the thousands of poems he'd written and picked out his favorites. He told a trusted friend about the haiku saying, "Maybe they have no value, but I'll see." Richard Wright died in 1960 at the age of fifty-two. His haiku were finally published in 1998 as a collection of 817 poems in a book titled *Haiku: This Other World.*

Would you like to write haiku? Take a look around you. Use all your senses. What do you see? What do you smell? What do you hear? How do you feel? **HAVE FUN!**

A NOTE ON THE ILLUSTRATIONS

While working on this book, I learned a few things about Richard Wright. I learned that he wanted readers to recognize and understand the experiences of African Americans. I learned that everyday sights and sounds of plants and animals, forests and farms inspired him when he was a little boy. I learned that he loved photography and took many photographs when he traveled. I am so pleased to illustrate his words with photographs. I photographed African American boys for this book, because I wanted the reader to imagine the world through a young brown boy's eyes. A boy, like Richard Wright, who found wonder in the world around him.

FURTHER READING

Ashley Bryan's ABC of African-American Poetry. New York: Atheneum Books for Young Readers, 1997. This celebration of African American writers brings together short poems and excerpts of longer poems with illustrations by Ashley Bryan.

Cleary, Brian P. *If It Rains Pancakes: Haiku and Lantern Poems.* Minneapolis: Millbrook Press, 2014. Learn more about two Japanese poetic forms—haiku and lantern poems—and read examples of both that range from thoughtful to just plain silly.

Hughes, Langston. *My People.* New York: Atheneum Books for Young Readers/Ginee Seo Books, 2009. A poem by Langston Hughes, an African American writer born just a few years before Richard Wright, is accompanied by photographs of contemporary African Americans taken by Charles R. Smith in this book for children.

Miller, William. *Richard Wright and the Library Card.* New York: Lee & Low Books, 1997. This picture book, illustrated by R. Gregory Christie, tells about how as a young man, Richard Wright wasn't allowed to borrow books from the library because of the color of his skin. Richard found a way around this restriction, thanks to a little help from a coworker.

Reibstein, Mark. *Wabi Sabi.* New York: Little, Brown, 2008. This story describes a cat's journey through Japan to understand the meaning of her name, Wabi Sabi. Haiku appear throughout this picture book, including some from classic Japanese poets Basho and Shiki.

Weatherford, Carole Boston. *Sugar Hill: Harlem's Historic Neighborhood.* Chicago: Albert Whitman, 2014. Poet Carole Boston Weatherford celebrates the writers, musicians, artists, and thinkers who were part of the Harlem Renaissance and the New York neighborhood at the center it. During Richard Wright's time in New York, he crossed paths with many of the people featured in this picture book.